ESSENTIAL CROWDFUNDING SUCCESS

KICKSTARTER INDIEGOGO

DO'S AND DON'TS

By

LIZ MOBI

Copyright © 2016

Book.CampaignFunded.com

Write.CampaignFunded.com

WHAT OTHERS ARE SAYING

Since I began using the Tips, others have shared them on their personal networks.

"I started getting a lot of hits and contributions on my campaign within days"

"I love this book, truly a great buy! Both Thumbs Up!"

"Absolutely Amazing. Anyone who is considering crowdfunding needs to read this book"

"Great book and an awesome author. They actually contributed to my campaign as well and gave me a lot of recommendations for my project. So appreciative"

For

My Five Heirs...

my Heirs Heirs...

my extended Heirs...

Every thing good I do is for

you and you and you...

INTRODUCTION

You have this great idea for an amazing product or business. You have a feeling that it will be the next big thing and your big break.

What happens? What stops you from going forward?

These two things likely:

1) Where to begin? How to turn an idea into a reality?

2) No Funds? How do you get the money to create this reality?

Crowdfunding has become a popular resource for funding ideas and products. Many entrepreneurs have been able to make dreams come true through sites like Kickstarter, Indiegogo, and similar platforms.

"You write a script, post it on a platform and watch the money start rolling in... right?"

Sounds simple enough? Not so fast! Recent stats from Kickstarter show a success rate of about 36%. Indiegogo and others have even lower success rates. That sounds pretty low but at the same time, it is over $2.1 billion in funding to almost 100 thousand projects.

As corny as it may sound, I wrote this book because I want everyone with a dream to be successful. You evidently have a dream or an idea that you think is pretty good and it led you here, trying to figure out how to turn your dream into a reality. I am here to tell you the steps to create and finance that Reality. I'll likely back your campaign as well.

Why I am a Crowdfunding Expert

Although the crowdfunding industry is relatively new, I do consider myself a Crowdfunding Expert.

My first project was a failure. Why? Because I was mesmerized by the home pages of Kickstarter & Indiegogo that featured campaigns that were funded, many of them two, three or more times over.

However, the good thing about my failure is I didn't just give up on crowdfunding. I watched it, studied it and pledged some of my own money to other projects. I learned exactly what it takes to go from an idea, to a project, to a Campaign Funded.

I am here to share the knowledge I have learned that puts all the puzzle pieces together so that one; you don't have to spend months on end searching and two; to direct you so your campaign ends in that success rate.

TABLE OF CONTENTS

Introduction

Table of Contents

Legal Notes

Chapter 1. A Bit About Crowdfunding

Chapter 2. Types of Crowdfunding

Chapter 3. Popular Sites

Chapter 4. Essential Crowdfunding Steps

Chapter 5. ZERO ($0) Funded NEVER

Chapter 6. Before You Launch

Chapter 7. An Effective Campaign

Chapter 8. Launching and Post Campaign

Chapter 9. Tips You Should Know

Chapter 10. Crowdfunding Secrets

About The Author

Legal Notes

All efforts have been made to produce the highest quality and informative book possible. No representations by the author should be construed as a guarantee from this information. Any examples in this material should not be interpreted as a promise.

All results are dependent on the person implementing the techniques and ideas that the author has described and explained. Results and level of success will vary per person depending on the time and actions they devote to the techniques and resources noted and will differ per individual.

By reading this you accept these terms and conditions.

All rights reserved. No part of this book may be reproduced or transmitted in any form or by any means, electronic or mechanical, including photocopying, recording or by any information storage and retrieval system, without written permission from the author, except for the inclusion of brief quotations in a review.

Chapter 1.
A Bit About Crowdfunding

Essentially, crowdfunding is "gathering a crowd" for monetary support.

Raising small amounts of money publicly from a large number of people amounts to widespread awareness. Online platforms provide a way to reach contributors / backers who are interested in financing businesses, projects and ventures in a public forum.

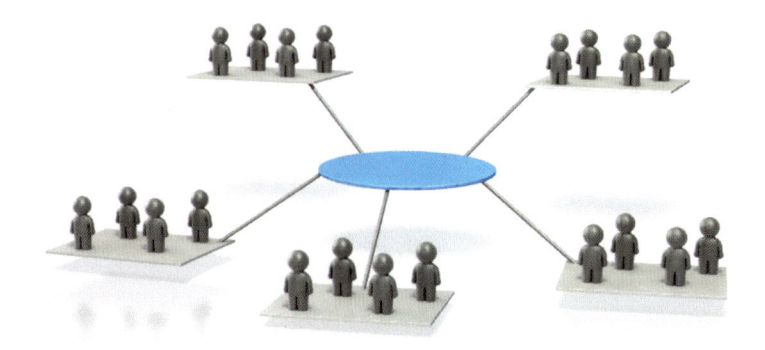

Crowdfunding being relatively new is a rapidly growing fundraising technique that has established itself as an alternative to traditional bank loans.

There are various types of crowdfunding platforms. In the ones we will explore here, the funds go directly to the creator, less fees from the platforms. The creator does not have to pay back the funds raised. There are also crowdfunding platforms where you borrow the funds but at a much lower rate than a bank.

There are a couple of ways to collect the funds.

"All or Nothing" means if you don't reach the goal set, you get nothing.

"Keep it All" means whatever you raise, you keep, regardless if you reach your goal.

Is Crowdfunding right for you?

As stated earlier, crowdfunding is not as simple as posting a campaign and watching the money roll in. Lots of work is involved. A successful campaign requires dedication, long hours and following my guidelines. With this, you have the steps to end up with a successfully funded campaign.

Pros	Cons
Test the market beforehand	Infringement
Build a customer base	Very public
Build your brand	No flexibility
Gain publicity	Overly successful
Get feedback	Delays in production
Fine tune your product	Lots of work
Don't pay back money	Paying fees on raised money

CHAPTER 2.
TYPES OF CROWDFUNDING

Crowdfunding is set up online. Sites are referred to as Platforms.

There are five avenues of crowdfunding:

Reward; Donation; Debt; Equity; and Royalty

This book focuses on the Reward and Donation platforms only. Both can be for business; individual projects; or causes, profit or non-profit organizations.

Reward	Keep 100% ownership of your project; no debt from the money raised; give rewards or perks related to your project in return for contribution such as T-shirts, DVDs, CDs, and more
Donation	Generally for causes, even personal. Thank you is given in return
Debt	Where the crowd (investors) lends money to businesses. Funds are paid back at a lower rate than from banks.
Equity	You receive shares for your investment, hoping for profits. Read the JOBS Act regarding restrictions.
Royalty	Contributors receive royalties or revenue when the project / product begins to generate sales.

REWARD / DONATION BASED

The **reward** base is the most popular type of crowdfunding. It is especially right for small business ventures as the funds raised are non-refundable and incentivize pledges with rewards such as gifts, media, samples, etc. It's a great opportunity to get creative. The value of the rewards depends on the amount of the contribution made. Rewards can be almost anything from a simple "thank you" to DVDs, T-shirts, digital graphics and items that are related to the campaign product or business.

The **donation** base allows backers to provide funds for nothing in return. *Why would they do this?* Generally, people donate because they believe in you or sympathize with your story. These backers contribute to your project, typically with small donations that can really add up fast.

Rewards cannot be offensive material, alcohol, contests, gambling, weapons, nothing illegal... there is a full list of prohibited items on most sites.

CHAPTER 3.

Popular Sites

GOFUNDME

DONATION – KEEP IT ALL

With over $1 billion in donations, individuals for personal fundraising and life events such as funerals, education, healthcare, pets, and more mostly use GoFundme. Non-profits have raised funds using GoFundme as well.

Aside from fees, all the money raised is yours to keep. Currently, fees are 5% & 2.9% + $.30 payment processing. Fees are slightly higher or lower in other countries and at 9.25% for charity organizations.

On GoFundme, there are no campaign time limits or rewards. The campaign can continue on and have recurring donations as well.

Now, why would someone just give you money and you received nothing in return? The answer is; there are people out here who just want to help others. It is important to write a heartwarming and sincere campaign pitch that others can empathize with.

This book outlines the steps to writing an effective campaign.

KICKSTARTER

REWARD – ALL OR NOTHING

Kickstarter is the most popular crowdfunding platform of them all and has raised over $2.2 billion in pledges. Kickstarter is an "All or Nothing" platform. This means that project creators set a limited time period and funding goal to reach (for example, one month and $5,000 goal). If you fully reach your goal with pledges from backers, you get the money. If the goal is not reached, then no funds are withdrawn from the backers' account.

Large, creative projects work well on Kickstarter. You will find filmmakers, musicians, artists, designers, writers, promoters and more presenting their idea or business venture in hopes of bringing their dreams to life. A rewards example would be; if you were interested in starting a small bakery, you could offer a reward of a dozen cookies for a pledge / donation.

Like GoFundme, all the money you collect is yours, no debt, less the site's fees currently at 5% & 3-5% payment processing. If you do not reach your goal, you collect nothing and there is no fee to you. Many feel Kickstarter is safer because they go through a strict process to verify your identity. Campaigns must be approved by Kickstarter.

INDIEGOGO

REWARD – ALL OR NOTHING & KEEP IT ALL

Indiegogo is a very well-known crowdfunding site and is very similar to Kickstarter with over $500 million raised. Indiegogo offers the "All or Nothing" option known as "Fixed Funding" goals but also offers the option to keep what you've raised called "Flex Funding" even if your goal is not met.

Indiegogo supports the same types of projects and has far more campaigns than Kickstarter, however the site does receives less traffic, fewer pledges and has a lower success rate.

Unlike Kickstarter, Indiegogo projects do not require approval. Funding can begin right away. The process of identification is not as stringent, which makes for fewer barriers to entry. Most projects that are denied by Kickstarter will go over to Indiegogo.

Indiegogo's pricing structure depends on how you decide to collect your funds. In general, total fees are between 8-10% for successful goals and an additional 4% for those where the goal is not reached. Indiegogo recently created a charity site called Generosity.com that is strictly for non-profits with no fee from them.

FIRSTGIVING

DONATION – KEEP IT ALL – NONPROFIT

Until recently, FirstGiving was strictly for non-profit organizations to fundraise for charities and various causes. Non-profits must be registered and verified with the IRS in order to start a campaign. Many well-known charities collect donations through FirstGiving.

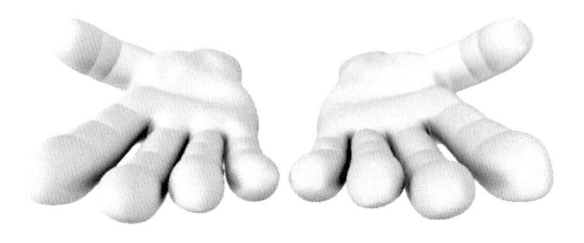

Personal Fundraising pages have recently become available for causes or to give directly to a charity of your choice. Campaigns can be ongoing and receive recurring donations from those who sign up. With FirstGiving, the campaign owner has the option to set up a payment schedule.

Fee structures vary with FirstGiving based on whether traditional crowdfunding using peer-to-peer giving or general donations are selected. Fees are from 4.25 to 7.50%, however there is an annual fee of $500 per year for a premium, non-profit account. FirstGiving claims you will raise more money using their platform.

MORE AND MORE SITES

Do a quick Google search and you'll find over a hundred various crowdfunding platforms.

CHAPTER 4.
ESSENTIAL CROWDFUNDING STEPS

The following are Essential Steps that are necessary and in this order to create a successful campaign.

1. **Build a Crowd** – Start three to six months prior
2. **Market Research & Contact** – Research sites and create lists of all contacts
3. **Professional Video** – First Impression Matters
4. **Campaign** – Effectively Written Campaign
5. **Rewards** – Critically Important
6. **Press Release** – Media Attention is Needed
7. **Campaign Launch** – It's not over
8. **Goal** – Campaign Funded – Post Launch

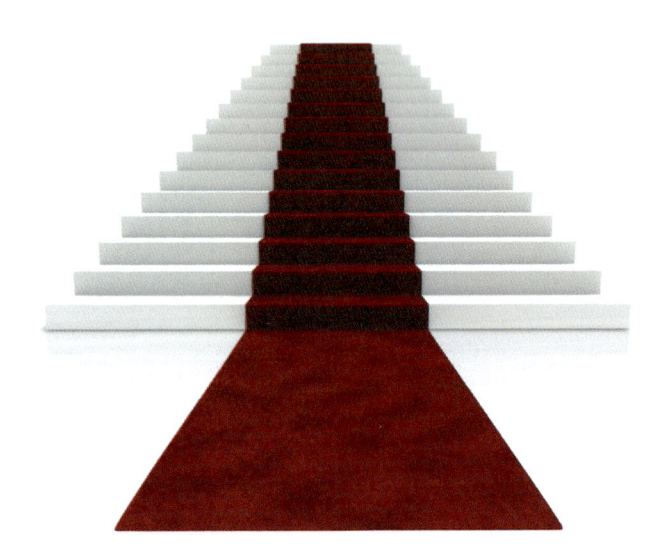

Do not expect the money to roll in as soon as your

campaign is posted. There is a strategy in having funds day one, but in most cases, a successful campaign takes work, building a crowd of backers and presenting a meaningful campaign or project that resonates with people, throughout the campaign.

Bottom line: these platforms are in business to make money. Successful campaigns are seen more easily through their search engines. The ones with the highest chance of success are being featured on homepages and being promoted by the platforms.

Backers will not come automatically, these essential steps lets them find you and you find them.

CHAPTER 5.
ZERO ($0) FUNDED - NEVER

An unsuccessful campaign with $0 dollars funded has to be the one of the most bizarre things ever seen on crowdfunding sites. Is the creator actually saying that they didn't have at least one friend or family member to donate at least one dollar to their cause? Seeing a creator with 800 Facebook friends, 1500 Twitter followers, yet not one person contributed. What about a page showing eight or less backers, how is this possible? A few reasons come to mind:

- They are not confident or embarrassed by their campaign.
- Trying to run a secret campaign, not wanting their name out in the public.
- They have no idea what they are doing.
- Something isn't quite connecting between the creator and the campaign process.
- Creator is not open or unwilling to listen to advice or criticism.

A zero funded campaign is ridiculous. Come on, you must call your mom, dad, sister, brother, aunt, cousin... someone to contribute. So seriously, even if you have to give them their dollar back ☺.

Quick Story regarding one of my points above: A creator requested consulting on a project where they wanted to provide help in Haiti. He wanted to have the *project on Kickstarter because he felt they had more visitors. Remember Kickstarter is reward based and he had none to offer. The creator also did not want to use his name, give no information about himself and basically had written one paragraph saying "please give me, a total stranger, money to provide help to Haiti even though I have no plan on how to provide this. I just have a heart to help." He was unwilling to accept that potential backers would not view his campaign as legitimate. In the end, he could not be verified by Kickstarter and ultimately went to GoFundme with the same information. "$0 Funded"*

CHAPTER 6.
BEFORE YOU LAUNCH

Become the expert about your product or business. Bonus points if you already are an expert. Do your homework by researching your product or idea. Know everything there is to know about what you are offering.

Hopefully you have an audience already, if not start building one now. It can take six months or more to build a viable audience and network of potential supporters who like you.

Social media accounts are highly important. Here is where it's extremely important to not be a lone person and having a team is good. Running multiple social network accounts takes a lot of time if you want to connect with your followers, get to know them socially and build a relationship with them BEFORE asking for money or posting about your campaign. If you already have a rapport established, they will be more willing to engage with your campaign.

At a minimum, three networks are a must: Facebook, Twitter and a blog. Instagram, Google+, LinkedIn, Pinterest and Reddit are other Networks worth joining as well finding niche sites similar to yours where you can contribute, comment, guest blog, do podcasts to gain traction and popularity for your campaign.

Anywhere you can build a relationship by adding your name can lead to a potential backer. Be sure to make your presence known, be everywhere, but be sure to engage conversation about other topics, not just about you or your project. Become "social friends" so that in six months, when you introduce your awesome campaign, people will want to support you.

About **30 days before your launch**, join pre-launch sites. These may or may not help but it does get your project out with a buzz in the media. Lots of marketing media sites will be contacting you for their marketing services. I don't have any I would recommend, as I haven't heard of any getting real good results. Don't just believe the reviews. Should you choose to pay for marketing, check their social network pages and make sure they communicate with their real followers. Contact other project owners and ask them it the marketing sites they use actually helped them.

Get a **Professional Press Release** written to announce your campaign. Find news sites / writers and send it to them. The more unique your project is, the higher chance of them posting it. Some sites offer free and paid postings. Check these sites out carefully before spending money on everyone who says they can help but do post on their free options. The more places you are the more you can get noticed.

Friends and Family Are Key

You should have a blog, website or landing page. Begin posting and sharing it with everyone. Ask friends to do a video testimony in support of your campaign and project, post it on your site as this adds much support and legitimacy. Create a worksheet with a timeline of what you are doing, your media connections; track the results and follow-up where you need to.

Contact local, neighborhood media outlets to post your story. Once a story is posted one place, link it everywhere, ask friends and family to comment on it, this can lead to it being posted other places and gets the word out.

Keep your friends and family apprised about the project, get their feedback to fine tune it, ask them to contribute on the first day of launch and leave a great comment. Remind them, be persistent, put your pride and ego away and get it done.

Finally, advertise and promote with a launch party. Invite people you've been communicating with, especially through meet-ups (join multiple groups). Launch party doesn't have to be big or fancy. Meet at a local restaurant/bar, order some appetizers and mingle for a couple of hours to create buzz, take pictures, post the pictures on your blog in a totally new article.

"Quick Story: A creator had an extremely well written campaign detailing her vision for an online platform for what she was teaching at the time. All the details were presented, the exact funds needed and how they would be used, great rewards were added, etc. She added videos showing her teaching students; images of what the online platform would look like. She launched her campaign and after a week or so, she only had a few backers. She did not understand why. Turns out, she did not do any pre-launch work; had not build up her crowd; wasn't active on social media, not even her personal Facebook page. No one knew about the campaign. Kickstarter didn't promote it. That creator was me ☹"

CHAPTER 7.
AN EFFECTIVE CAMPAIGN

A good Campaign Pitch starts with the video. As the first thing potential backers see, you must introduce yourself and be confident. Create a professional, high quality video that is to-the-point and demonstrates to potential backers what your campaign is all about.

The **Video** should be:

- No longer than 2-3 minutes, I suggest 2
- Should be memorable, exciting and tells potential backers
    - Who you are
    - What your idea or product is and does
    - Why they should support and back your campaign

The **Pitch** should:

- Get to the point within the first two paragraphs
- Detail what your idea or project is
- Tell your intentions

After the first two paragraphs, you can begin to give more details, and then begin to tell your "story".

The **Story** should:

- Be sincere, clear and credible
- Share how you arrived at this point
- What your plans are with your project.

- Convince them you know your product thoroughly
- Share your experience or expertise on the product or business
- Explain how you will bring it to fruition.

Backers will not only be investing in your product, they will be investing in you as well. Convince them that you are worth it.

Do include quality, high-resolution images of you and your product (good animation is a plus).

The **Goal** amount:

- Not too high
- Set a realistic goal of the minimum amount you need to successfully meet your campaign
- Assess how much you need to get the ball rolling to the next step. For example, a lower goal of $5,000 is more attainable than a $50,000 goal.
    - However, you must fulfill the campaign and rewards.
    - After lower goals are reached, stretch goals can be added and promoted until the end of the campaign or
    - Consider a second campaign.

Your campaign must be well written, error-free using proper grammar and a reasonable length. Answer the old *"Who, What, When, Where and How"*!

REWARDS

The best rewards are tangible, realistic and are guaranteed deliverable. Your backers want and will appreciate something in return. There are ways to reward even the smallest backer. Perhaps the reward for a $1 donations is including their name in a list on your website. Make sure you give practical items that are 100% deliverable.

Reward examples:

    A musician raising funds for his album provides physical autographed album covers.

    A chef offers backers an opportunity to name or vote on a flavor of sauce that he is crowdfunding for.

Have several rewards, a good number is between 4 and 8 levels. The key is not to overdo it, which can confuse your backer. It is easy to get carried away but note that a common midlevel and mostly taken award is $25 - $30. Other considerations include an early bird reward and post-goal rewards to capitalize on the momentum. Always have a $1 reward level so that potential backers are aware that they can donate at small amounts. Offer a sincere thank you, digital high-five or a mention on your website.

Determine the reward delivery dates and deliver on time. People who have entrusted their hard-earned money expect you to meet reward deadlines.

Quick Story: An amazing campaign for a group of excited friends was launched. It was very detailed and well written. The friends had some strange but interesting spices to introduce to the world. Their video was professionally done and featured a party of them trying out the spice product, everyone was laughing and having fun. Anyone watching this video would want to be at that party and try those spices. Great rewards were set up and the campaign was a hit. Very successful and surpassed its goal. There were still a few of issues. One was the creator set the cost of the rewards too low after everything was calculated. Second, they did not calculate the shipping cost for which they ended up having to pay out more, especially with the international shipping. Third, there were a few lost shipments that were replaced, causing more unexpected expenses. Lastly, the creators really hadn't anticipated having such a huge success. Strangely enough, had they only made goal and not three times over, they wouldn't have had to go into their own pockets in the end to complete the rewards. In the end, the friends did launch a new business but they were already in the red, in debt. Setting proper goals, reward pricing and shipping costs are crucial especially when you have a successful campaign and always "plan for success".

RISKS AND CHALLENGES

Outline the anticipated risks and challenges you may face in completing the campaign. In the event of a challenge, detail how you will overcome should it arise. Your campaign should convince any potential backer that your product or idea can be trusted and is worth financial backing. Also, ensure that you are someone that your backers can have confidence in.

You may feel that your campaign will go off without a glitch so no risks need to be noted. Be careful with that, as backers are extremely smart and have examined various campaigns. We tend to look at creators who expect no risk to not be realistic; everything has risks so include at least one risk, even a minor risk.

Chapter 8.
Launching and Post Campaign

Launching Your Campaign

With everything in order, all you need to do is push the launch button and your campaign begins at that moment. Providing you've completed all the plenaries, especially with Kickstarter who can take up to three days to review and make sure your campaign falls within their guidelines of a project. Also, that you've verified who you are and your banking information so that funds can be sent to you when it's over.

Now remember the work does not end here. Follow-up with friends and family to contribute now, the first day is crucial. Get heavy on social media and let everyone know the time has come, ask them to contribute, send email reminders and be sure not to spam anyone. Your project can be deleted for spam.

Fun fact: Stats show that the best day to launch is on a Monday.

Fun fact: Crowdfunding projects with duration of 30 days seem to reach their goal more than others.

Managing Your Campaign

Check the stats on the funding site you are using. Pay attention to where you are getting the most traffic and target those areas you are relating to.

Continue to be social friends and not someone who posts about money all day long. Know that this is a full time commitment and every part of the process is continual, including pre-launch activities to keep your campaign gaining more backers. By now you should know more of your target areas to focus on. Be sure to thank everyone, respond and expound on their comments they leave, do interviews, guest podcasts, and continue to work on the progress of the product. Prepare for success.

Update your campaign's progress frequently, at least once a week.

Post Launch

After you have a successful Campaign Funded, the hard work now begins...

Now it is time to begin the work you have been waiting for. Typically, it takes at least 30 days to receive the funds from a project. In the meantime, accomplish all that you can possible do without actually having the funds.

Again I stress, deliver rewards on time per your reward dates. Backers will get upset if you fail to deliver on time and will post negative comments. If you are experiencing issues with delivery, inform your backers. Begin your new journey and don't forget about the platform and backers. They may be lifelong supporters and with platforms now adding the option to continue ordering from the campaign page after the project period is over, it is essential to have a great reputation. Do not burn those bridges.

Chapter 9.
Tips You Should Know

1. Do not expect the money to roll in as soon as your campaign is posted. A successful campaign takes work, building a crowd of backers, and presenting a meaningful campaign or project that resonates with people. You must use targeted marketing on your audience without spamming.
The Bottom line: These platforms are in business to make money. Successful campaigns with backers are being discovered easily through their search engines. The ones with the highest chance of success are being featured on homepages and are being promoted by the platforms. Backers will not come automatically. You will need to bring backers to you first so platforms will want to display yours.

2. Before you begin, spend time browsing crowdfunding sites. Look at various categories, especially your type. Analyze successful and failed campaigns. Discover why some reached goal and others failed. Now you should have a good idea and can implement the best of what you learned into your campaign.

3. Record a video that is professional and high quality. Campaigns using videos that show real people, human beings with personality are best. Backers love this.
4. Getting family and friends to pledge right away is key. When you can demonstrate support early on, it gives you a great start. (see secret)
5. Post frequent updates about your campaign and communicate. If someone comments on your campaign, respond always, expound on their comment and accept their feedback.
6. Draft a Press Release and send it to media outlets. A professional written Press Release is best, as it will have all the essential information on it and connects with the readers.

CHAPTER 10.
CROWDFUNDING SECRETS

- All-or-Nothing projects get more funding and backers than Keep-it-All. You may be tempted to for the Keep-it-all but know that backers tend to question whether to give to this type projects in fear of the creator being unable to complete the project so no rewards and a loss of funds to the backers.
- Donate to other campaigns before and during your campaign, especially those campaigns that show they have backed other campaigns (check their profile). Those owners often feel obligated to reciprocate. Potential backers see that as a good deed and some who is also willing to help others. This means a lot to potential backer and many will back you based on that. (I do)
- Gather a team. Teams have a better rate of reaching their goal than single creators adding to the legitimacy factor of the campaign. It shows potential backer that others are vouching for you. Try to get two or three others to be involved in your project.

- No platform will admit this, but generally if your campaign receives 50 or more backers during a 24-36 hour period (best at the start), it will bring your campaign to the front of the listings, resulting in hundreds of thousands of potential backer views. Next step perhaps "Staff Pick," "Projects We Love," "Top Picks," or "Trending" features. This is a primary reason it is important to secure the support of your friends and family to pledge / **contribute on Day One**.

Now go forth and be prosperous.

About The Author
AUTHOR NAME is Liz Mobi

"I looked up and all of a sudden I noticed that I had become a Serial Crowdfunding Backer. Seems it happened overnight. With my contributions given to various campaigns, I have learned so much about crowdfunding and how to be successful. I soon began giving advice on what works and what doesn't. Now within seconds, I can easily give tips.

So, I decided to write and publish my first book. This is so I can help others get their Campaign Funded Successfully. And guess what? The serial backer continues, you have purchased my book and I will back your campaign as well. Send me a message from my website for details.

I have specific documents that are extremely helpful for these Essential Steps available on my website and continue to add more. Please go to Write.CampaignFunded.com

Liz

CAN I ASK A FAVOR?

If you enjoyed this book, found it useful or otherwise then I'd really appreciate it if you would post a short review on Amazon. I do read all the reviews personally so that I can continually write what people are wanting and need.

If you'd like to leave a review then please visit the link below:

Also, I am very interested in seeing how your campaign turns out. Please send me a link and as you know, I am still a serial backer so don't be surprised if I back your project.

Thanks for your support!

Printed in Great Britain
by Amazon